Every Day Is a Good Day

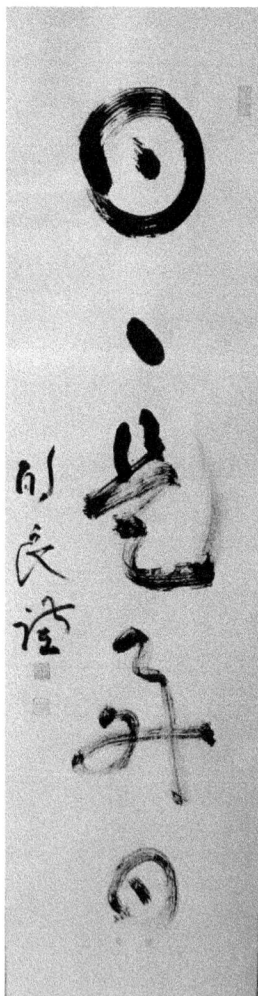

Every Day Is a Good Day

DAVID H. ROSEN

RESOURCE *Publications* · Eugene, Oregon

EVERY DAY IS A GOOD DAY

Resource Publications
An Imprint of Wipf and Stock Publishers
199 W. 8th Ave., Suite 3
Eugene, OR 97401

www.wipfandstock.com

PAPERBACK ISBN: 978-1-7252-6821-0
HARDCOVER ISBN: 978-1-7252-6822-7
EBOOK ISBN: 978-1-7252-6823-4

Manufactured in the U.S.A.   04/09/20

OTHER WORKS BY DAVID H. ROSEN

Scholarly

Medicine as a Human Experience (with David Reiser)
Patient-Centered Medicine: A Human Experience (With Uyen Hoang)
Soul Circles: Mandalas and Meaning
The Tao of Elvis
The Tao of Jung: The Way of Integrity
Transforming Depression: Healing the Soul Through Creativity

Collections of Haiku

Clouds and More Clouds
The Healing Spirit of Haiku (With Joel Weishaus)
In Search of the Hidden Pond
Living with Evergreens
Look Closely
Spelunking through Life
Torii Haiku: Profane to a Sacred Life
Warming to Gold: A Collection of Haiku
White Rose, Red Rose: A Collection of Haiku (with Johnny Baranski)

Memoir

Lost in the Long White Cloud: Finding My Way Home
Torn Asunder: Putting Back the Pieces (forthcoming)

Children's Books

Henry's Tower
Kindergarten Symphony: An ABC Book
Samantha the Sleuth & Zack's Hard Lesson
Time, Love, and Licorice: A Healing Coloring Story Book

Miscellaneous

The Alchemy of Cooking: Recipes with a Jungian Twist
Opal Whiteley's Beginning and Hoops and Hoopla

Preface

THE TITLE OF THIS collection comes from Natsume Sōseki. Sōseki was a well-known Japanese author of novels, haiku, and fairytales, as well as a calligrapher and painter, whose most famous works include, I am a Cat and Light and Darkness. In Zen and Haiku, a collection of his poems and letters, Sōseki finishes a playful retelling of a well-known Zen dialogue by using the phrase: "Every day is a good day." Years after this book was given to me by a Japanese friend and colleague, I found a scroll with this Zen phrase (included as the frontispiece) in the back corner of a scroll shop in the old city of Kyoto Japan. It has hung in my home for many years.

The seeds of these haiku were planted during my visits to Japan (with its swaying bamboo and sculpted cliffs), but they also lead readers through my journey encompassing health and illness. Every day really is a good day: but some days one enjoys the seasons, the red moon, and wildflowers, and some days one suffers the frustration and pains of aging. We are not accustomed to seeing both kinds of days as good, but there really is an art to be found in aches and pains, as much as love and tenderness. Accepting both, appreciating both, is an ongoing part of our awakening.

PART I

Learning from Travels

JAPAN

Sun on Nihon sea
swaying bamboo
sculpted cliffs

Kokoro
here, there . . .
everywhere

GREECE

Walk through olive groves
a peaceful silence . . .
wildflowers everywhere

Ancient Andritsaina
Temple of Apollo
soul among pillars

FINLAND

Sauna before dinner
snow and striking birch branches
Marja and I take our time

SOUTH AFRICA

Zen zebras . . .
our future

GREENLAND

Red moon sets
over Greenland . . .
climate change

OREGON, UNITED STATES

In the red rose
a bumble bee . . .
that was close

Fall is here
orange red leaves
wild turkeys gobble

No way
in or out
but love is here

Cold wind
while we wait . . .
warming up

NEW ZEALAND

Sunset
Over
Unique
Love

Trust enables
wholeness . . .
human mandalas

TRAVELING THROUGH IMAGINATION

Sleepy sloth
shy and stoic
strong swimmer

PART II

The Doctor Learns
from Illness

MS AS TEACHER

My Sunrise
My Shock
My Soul
My Sanity
My Strength
My Setback
My Solitude
My Star
My Sloth
My Sage

DEEP BLUE

Still the same person,
moving slow . . .
MS

The sky deep blue,
misty clouds . . .
MS

Butte in the distance,
birdsong . . .
MS

MS AS GUIDE

Muse by my Side
creation from pain
writing at night

OLD MAN WANDERING

Old man wandering
in a young night . . .
will he make it or not?

Old man wandering
in a young night . . .
"come in dear."

Old man wandering
in a young night . . .
love says, "I'm here."

Old man wandering
in a young night . . .
sees something, but what?

Old man wandering
in a young night . . .
looking down, then up.

Old man wandering
in a young night . . .
wife by his side.

THE ART OF SUFFERING

I bow my head in shame
for all the killings of self and other.

I bow my head in sorrow
for inner and outer wars.

I bow my head in suffering
for all the tragedy that exists.

I bow my head in synchronicity
for we are all the same.

I bow my head in surrender
as it leads to acceptance.

I bow my head in prayer
since it is all we have.

I bow my head in love
as that is all we need.

I bow my head in ecstasy
to balance all the agony.

I bow my head in peace
and everlasting gratitude.

GODOT

Handicapped,
disabled space . . .
waiting for Godot